Dr. Seymour Kindbud

the
BONG
BIBLE

The Definitive DIY Guide to Pipes of All Shapes & Sizes

CIDER MILL
PRESS

BOOK
PUBLISHERS

13-Digit ISBN: 978-1-60433-234-6
10-Digit ISBN: 1-60433-234-4

This book may be ordered by mail from the publisher. Please include $2.95 for postage and handling. Please support your local bookseller first!

Books published by Cider Mill Press Book Publishers are available at special discounts for bulk purchases in the United States by corporations, institutions, and other organizations. For more information, please contact the publisher.

Cider Mill Press Book Publishers
"Where good books are ready for press"
12 Port Farm Road
Kennebunkport, Maine 04046

Visit us on the Web!
www.cidermillpress.com

Design by Melissa Gerber
All illustrations courtesy of Shutterstock.com and Melissa Gerber

Printed in China

1 2 3 4 5 6 7 8 9 0
First Edition

DISCLAIMER:
Do not play with matches or any fire-related devices. You may get burned. Do not smoke—it is not healthy. If smoking certain substances is illegal where you live, either move or don't smoke those substances. You could get arrested, and jail is not healthy. Consider yourself warned that the material in this book is for educational, historical, and medical purposes only. So, to recap: we do not condone smoking or breaking the law or going to jail. All are bad.

CONTENTS

INTRODUCTION

Whether you live in a condo or on a farm, with your mother or a college dorm-mate, *The Bong Bible* is here as your number-one resource for all things water pipe related. This book holds information key to unlocking the full stoner potential of everyday items surrounding you. You may appreciate the high, but you're also an inventor and artist! Now get to work turning some ordinary household items into pieces of functioning art. You'll not only impress your friends, but you'll be setting a good example by recycling all sorts of things that would normally end up tossed in the trash.

This book not only includes tons of do-it-yourself pipe projects with color photographs, but also a reference section, some interesting history, tips and tricks, hilarious and inspiring quotations, and more! We've also included some DIY non-water pipes and other methods of intake for your enjoyment.

So what are you waiting for? Get working and start smoking!

WARNING
& CAUTION

Please use common sense when using a homemade bong or pipe. Don't inhale burning or melting plastics or other materials that contain toxins. Some metals such as aluminum from cola cans and metal pieces from the hardware store are unsafe to inhale. If you're going to smoke out of a can, at least scrape off the paint before putting a flame to it. Also, be careful not burn yourself or someone else or set anything on fire. With the given imperfections of any homemade project, there are inconsistencies that can make one pipe work well and another, made of the same design, function poorly or dangerously. So be careful! Also, remember to rinse all containers thoroughly before building the projects in this book.

HISTORY & PHYSICS OF THE BONG

The Origin

The modern term "bong" comes from the Thai word *baung* meaning a cylindrical container cut from a bamboo stem to be used as a pipe. In 1944, the *McFarland Thai-English Dictionary* published one of the meanings of the word as "a bamboo water pipe for smoking kancha, tree, hashish, or the hemp-plant."

The term began to be used widely in the United States in the 1970s. During the Vietnam War, American soldiers stationed in Thailand took up the local's practice of smoking cannabis out of baung pipes. When the troops returned home they brought the term back with them, transforming it along the way into "bong."

Today bongs come in all shapes, sizes, and varieties. When walking into a store to check some out, make sure you refer to them as "water pipes" or you may not be welcome.

Components & Physics of a Bong

A water pipe, or bong, is made up of three simple components.

1. The bowl/stem, in which you put your smoking product.
2. The main chamber, which is partially filled with liquid.
3. A mouthpiece, which you inhale from.
4. Many water pipes also have a carburetor, or carb, which is a secondary air supply into the main chamber, which is used to clear the smoke.

There are many variations and additions one can make, such as additional chambers, ice catchers, and sliding male and female bowl/stem pieces.

The physics of a bong are fairly simple. As your mouth draws air through the mouthpiece, air is pulled through the bowl, through the slide

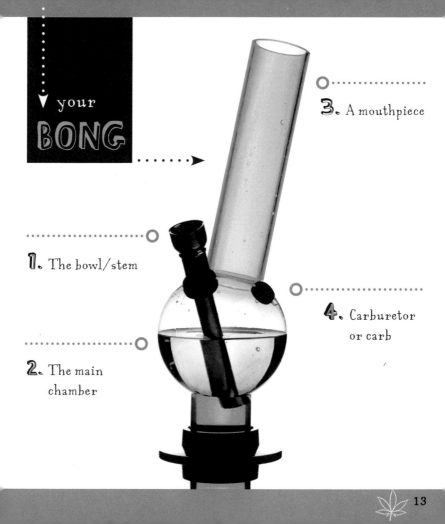

your
BONG

3. A mouthpiece

1. The bowl/stem

2. The main chamber

4. Carburetor or carb

13

(or other connector), into the water in the main chamber and then up to your mouth. It is vital to your bong's functionality to have airtight seals at all your junctions.

▼ the
BUBBLEGUM SAVE

Sometimes a homemade pipe's seal weakens with time. (Or perhaps it wasn't incredibly strong to begin with.) Don't be afraid to put a little chewed bubblegum around the leaking junction to create an airtight seal. Just don't smoke any burning bubblegum!

Why Water?

So, why do you need water in a bong? Water acts as a cleaning filter that cools the smoke as it runs through it. Sometimes other liquids can be used, and usually at some point (usually in a college dorm room), someone will have the tremendous idea of using cola or alcohol instead of water. They don't usually do it a second time. Why? It doesn't heighten the moment, and it isn't worth the time and effort needed to clean the bong afterward. As for alcohol, you may enjoy the taste, but since THC is alcohol soluble, you're actually receiving less THC. Talk about buzz kill—unless you drink the alcohol, of course.

It may look tempting, but water's best.
· ·➤

Types of Bongs

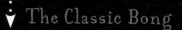

The Classic Bong

The classical bong is made up of a vertical tubular chamber that is partially filled with water, a bowl whose stem goes into the water, and a mouthpiece or opening at the top of the tube. . . . .

The Slide Bong

The slide bong is the same as the classical bong except that the bowl is attached to a glass slide that is used to clear the pipe.

CLASSIC

17

The Bubbler

The bubbler is another variation on the classic bong in which a carb is used to clear the pipe. Many bubblers are horizontal in design.

Gravity/Waterfall

A gravity bong uses water and gravity to draw smoke into a container. These can be made in many variations. The basic physics involves submerging a container in water and then displacing the water out a secondary hole to create airflow through a smoking bowl. A waterfall bong is a variation on a gravity bong where the water is released as a waterfall out the bottom of the container to draw smoke into the chamber.

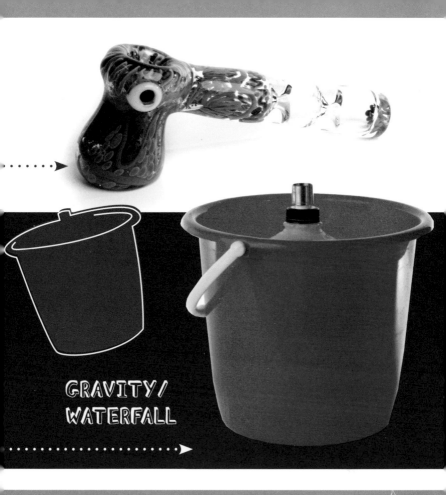

GRAVITY/
WATERFALL

19

Hookah

A hookah is a tobacco pipe originating from the East. Smoke is drawn through a chamber with water in it and into a long tube with a mouthpiece at the end. Some hookahs have multiple tubes so that more than one smoker may partake at the same time.

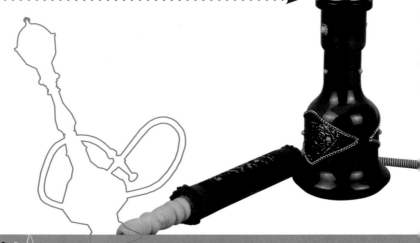

Non-Bong Intake Methods

▼ Classic Pipe

A classic pipe is much like a bong, but contains no water component. The most basic classic pipes have a bowl and a mouthpiece. Many have an added carb and other features such as color-changing glass.

Rush Tube

A rush tube is a long cylindrical tube that is used to inhale large amounts of smoke quickly.

You can easily turn a didgeridoo into a rush tube—see page 133

Vaporizer

A vaporizer uses a precision-controlled heating element to heat herbs to the point where THC is extracted in vapor form. The herbs are not actually burned thus saving the smoker from inhaling carcinogenic matter. The heating element is attached to a bowl that fills a bag or receptacle with the vapor.

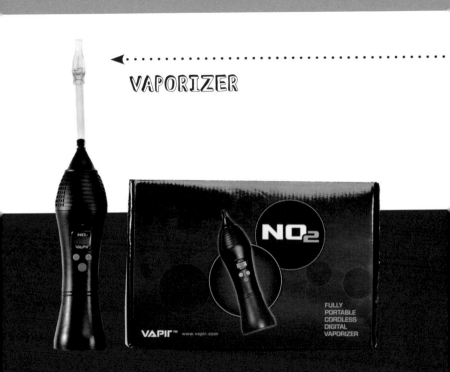

VAPORIZER

The Vapir NO2 vaporizer is a great portable option. It can run off a
battery and has replaceable mouthpieces.

Hot Knives

"Hot knives" is a method used to smoke hash. Two knives are heated on a stove (or other heating element). Once hot, a piece of hash is placed on one knife and then covered with the other. The sandwiched hash will begin to smoke and is usually just inhaled by holding the knives close to the mouth.

Edibles

THC, the main active substance in marijuana, may be extracted into oil or butter and used for baking and cooking.

HOT KNIVES

EDIBLES

25

Alcohol

THC is alcohol soluble. In some lands this drink is produced freely.

▼ Don't Get Kicked Out of the
HEAD SHOP!

Until herb is legalized here is a list of translations to insure happy shopping:

Home:	Store:
Bong *(n)*	Water Pipe
Bowl *(n)*	Pipe
Marijuana *(n)*	Tobacco
Hit *(v, n)*	to smoke, or a single inhalation
High *(adj)*	Happy
Session *(n)*	Party

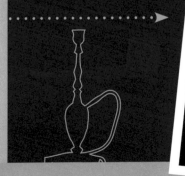

DO-IT-YOURSELF TOOLS

cut here

General Tools You'll Want on Hand

Some projects are more in-depth than others, but here are some tools that will come in handy while constructing your masterpieces.

- Scissors
- Razor blade
- Leatherman multi-tool
- Drill (with diamond-tip bit if working with glass)
- Different varieties of tape (duct, pipe-sealing Teflon, electrical, etc.)
- Paperclips

Making the Slide or Bowl

There are many different options when selecting what to use for your bowl and stem. There are homemade methods that can be made with commonly found items at your hardware store. There are also store-bought alternatives such as a glass slide and stem, which you can purchase from your local head shop or online. There are a few basic DIY ways illustrated here, but the sky's the limit. Be creative and fashion your own or use a store-bought glass slide if you prefer.

The Homemade Stem

There are many ways to construct a homemade bowl/stem piece. We have found that a trip to your local hardware store will provide you with many options. As you're walking the aisles, keep your eye out for anything resembling a bowl piece. Generally the plumbing fixtures area is a good place to start. One of the best tools in your DIY belt will be plastic aquarium tubing. You can basically connect anything with the tubing, and it provides an airtight seal.

For the projects in this book, we often used this piece for our bowls. It's technical name is the PEX plumbing fitting #C-PEX W F 1807 UPC cNSFus-pw. Try saying that five times fast.

HARDWARE STORE SCAVENGER HUNT

- For an ice-catcher carb mouthpiece check out: 1 1/2'" Plumb Pak 32-8WK

- For a curved mouthpiece check out: Cantex ½" non-metallic conduit elbow

- PVC pipes and joints of all shapes and sizes work great.

- Sure, your mom may have noticed that those little metal screens inside the faucet keep disappearing, but will she ever really catch on? These screens, also sold in hardware stores (separately and in bulk) and many tobacco shops, are one of the best tools in a home inventor's stock. Place one inside your bowl to insure no one will be eating ash and also to prevent good bud from going down the "drain" prematurely.

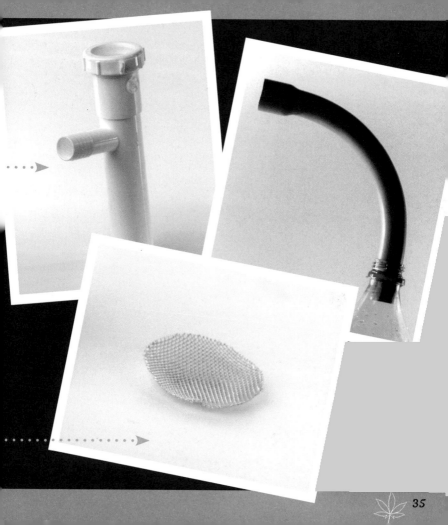

Store-Bought Slide

Using a store-bought slide can really spruce up your DIY pipe. Using a male/female slide set gives you a built-in method of clearing the smoke out of the chamber, and with the rubber washers, it gives your pipe an airtight seal. Any stem with a male/female slide piece can be used as the bowl as well as the carb. After adding your tobacco, you hold a flame above the packed bowl as you inhale through the mouthpiece. Once the chamber has filled with the desired amount of smoke, you slide the male bowl component out of the female and continue to inhale. This will rush fresh air into the pipe, sending the smoke into your lungs.

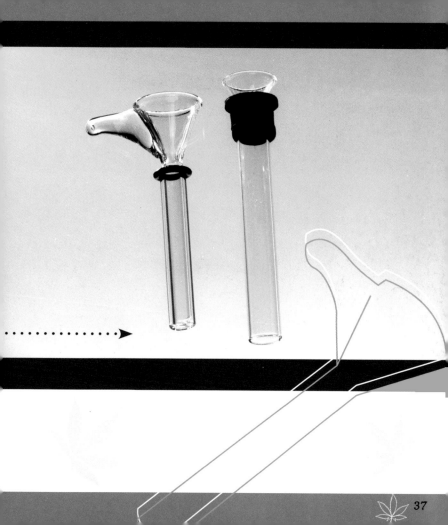

▼ Store-Bought Smoke 'n' Poke

The Smoke n' Poke is a great affordable tool that turns any plastic bottle into a water pipe. It travels very easily, making it great to take to parties.

Check out this water bottle. One quick poke with a Smoke 'n' Poke, and the bottle is instantly transformed.

Cleaning Up

It is a good idea to clean your glass pipes every so often. As smoke passes through the glass, it deposits small amounts of resin along the interior surfaces of the pipe. After a while this can lead to clogged pipes and funky tastes and smells when using the pipe. To clean your pipe, simply submerge it in a glass-cleaning solution for an hour or more (depending on how dirty the pipe is), remove, and then rinse off.

Purple Power Original Liquid Glass Cleaning Formula

This is a great alternative to standing over the sink for hours scrubbing your glass. Simply fill the receptacle with Purple Power, submerge your pipes, and let them soak.

THE PROJECTS

Incredible Edibles

The Apple Pipe

This is a classic that many smokers who find themselves stranded can use. You use the hollow shaft of a pen to make the holes in the apple. You can use a screen so you don't lose any product, but it's not required. As always wash everything before use.

BUILD TIME ✳ 5 MINUTES

MATERIALS ◄······················

Apple
Hollow pen shaft
Screen

DIRECTIONS

1. Use the pen shaft to create a hole along one side of the apple to the center.

2. Create a second hole, 90 degrees to the first hole, ending in the center so that both holes meet.

3. Remove the apple stem.

4. Create a third hole where the stem joined the first two holes (in the center of the apple).

5. Place the screen on top of the stem hole, and you're good to go.

There is no benefit to eating your edible pipes, except for the recycling aspect. If a smoker is set on eating their pipe, they should rinse it before consumption.

The Bell Pepper Bong

Leading its class in disposable bongs, the bell pepper bong is sure to impress your guests. By using our recommended ice-catcher carb mouthpiece, you'll have an ice-catcher and a carb built into the one component. The carb tube is located about one-third of the way down the tube and creates a shelf that will hold an ice cube for cool smoking.

BUILD TIME ✳ 5 MINUTES

MATERIALS

Bell pepper
Poke 'n' Smoke (see page 38)
Ice-catcher carb mouthpiece (see page 34)
Ice cube

DIRECTIONS

1. Cut a hole around the pepper stem so the circumference will fit the ice-catcher carb mouthpiece.

2. Rinse out the inside of the pepper and discard any loose seeds.

3. Fill the pepper one-third full with water.

4. Insert the Poke 'n' Smoke in the middle of the pepper as shown in the photograph.

5. Insert the mouthpiece partially into the top hole.

6. Before inserting the mouthpiece into its final position, wrap a little Teflon tape around the area that will touch the pepper to insure an airtight seal.

7. Place an ice cube into the mouthpiece — it should get stuck about halfway down the tube.

The Never-Bored Gourd Pipe

This pipe is awesome for all the autumn holidays. Not only does it blend into your surrounding fall display, but it also puts everyone in a really good mood. We used a cigar tube and a hollow pen shaft for our carb and mouthpiece, but feel free to use whatever you have laying around.

BUILD TIME ✳ 10 MINUTES

MATERIALS

Small pumpkin or other gourd
Hollow pen shaft
Blunt tube
Bowl piece
Screen

DIRECTIONS

1. Create two holes, one on either side of the gourd, which connect in the middle.

2. Insert the pen shaft into the hole furthest from you and the blunt tube into the opposite hole.

3. Create a hole on the top of the gourd that connects to the airshaft and secure the bowl piece in it.

Vertical Gourd Bong

This vegetable looks so much like a bong it's impossible to resist. It's a little difficult to work with, but it's so worth it.

BUILD TIME ✽ 10 MINUTES

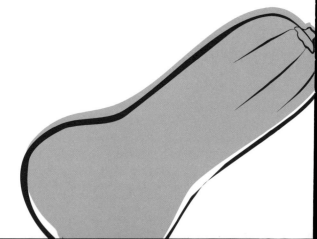

Gourd

Male/female slide set (see page 36)

DIRECTIONS ....

1. Cut the top off the gourd (as you would a pumpkin).
2. Core a shaft through the meat of the top section until you reach the hollow lower chamber.
3. Make a hole on the lower portion that your slide will go in.
4. Add water and you're ready to go.

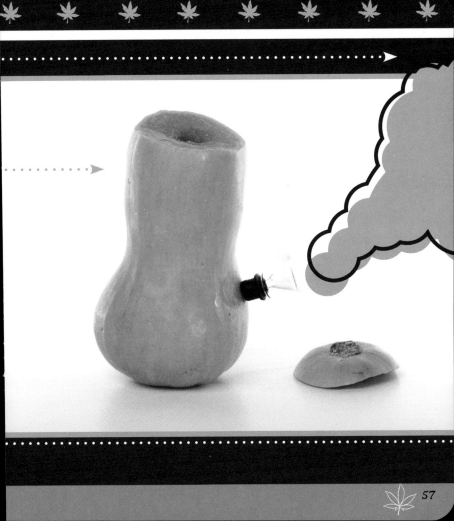

CocoNUT Bong

Feeling tropical? A coconut is excellent for creating an airtight seal, and it's easy to hold. Be careful not to split your coconut when creating the holes.

BUILD TIME ✳ 15 MINUTES

MATERIALS

Coconut
Male/female slide set (see page 36)
Small piece of aquarium tubing
Drill

DIRECTIONS

1. Drill two holes in the coconut, one on the top and one on the side. See the photograph for placement of the holes.
2. Drain the coconut milk.
3. Fit the slide into the side hole.
4. Fill the coconut up one-third full with water.
5. Fit the tubing into top hole—this is your mouthpiece.

The Spud-tacular Pipe

If you don't have an apple lying around, don't fret. Try this Mr. Potato Head-Shop.

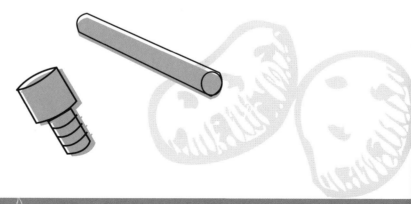

Potato
Hollow pen shaft (which you will cut in half after making your holes)
Bowl piece
Screen

DIRECTIONS ································

1. Push the hollow pen shaft through the potato lengthwise to create a shaft running the entire length of the potato. You should have a hole through both ends now.

2. Remove the pen shaft and make a third hole on top of the potato that connects to the shaft.

3. Twist your bowl piece into the top hole.

4. Cut the pen shaft in half and put one in each of the first two holes so that some of each shaft is protruding.

The Pineapple Bong

Here's another tropical treat. You'll get a great taste through this pipe.

BUILD TIME ✳ 10 MINUTES

MATERIALS

Pineapple
Male/female slide set (see page 36)
Elbow conduit

DIRECTIONS ....

1. Cut the top of the pineapple off, creating a flat surface.
2. Core the center of the pineapple to the diameter of the elbow conduit, leaving an inch or two at the base.
3. Create a hole for the slide about halfway up the pineapple and insert the slide.
4. Fill the pineapple one-third of the way up with water.
5. Insert the elbow conduit into the top of the pineapple and make sure it's sealed.

Things to Put
IN YOUR BONG (BESIDES POT)

- Try putting a couple of ice cubes into your bong to get a fresh, cool hit. Check out some pro bongs online or at the local head shop. Some bongs have coils built into the pipe, which you can freeze for the same effect.

- Many smokers have enjoyed substituting brandy instead of water in their bong. If you like brandy, give it a try. Since THC is soluble in alcohol you'll be trading a little THC for flavor. But you can always drink the brandy!

- Salvia divinorum: Still legal, still hallucinogenic.

- There are tons of great flavored tobaccos. Don't forget to check them out.

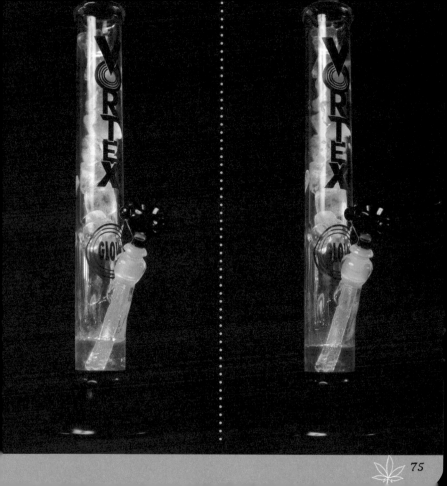

Household Helpers

Honey Bear Bong

This is a classic known to just about every smoker (who likes honey). There are many variations of this pipe. We included a carb and decided to make the original top the mouthpiece.

BUILD TIME ✳ 10 MINUTES

MATERIALS ·····························➤

Empty honey bear bottle
Bowl piece
Screen
Teflon tape
2 short lengths of aquarium tubing, one slightly longer than the other

DIRECTIONS ·····························

1. Create a hole in the front center of the honey bear.
2. Fill the honey bear with water up to the hole you just created.
3. Connect the longer piece of vinyl tubing to the end of the bowl piece.
4. Wrap the threads of the bowl piece in Teflon tape, feed the tubing into the hole in the honey bear, and twist the bowl into the hole so that the tube will reach the water.
5. Create a second hole on the back of the honey bear, well above the front hole.
6. Insert the smaller vinyl tubing into the back hole so a little is protruding. The cap is your mouthpiece.

Tequila Bong

Here's a bong you can make from your favorite brand of tequila (or anything else as long as the bottle looks cool). We found mini Patron bottles work great for the standard slide diameter.

BUILD TIME ✳ 15 MINUTES

MATERIALS

Glass bottle
Aquarium tubing
Male/female slide set (see page 36)
Diamond-coated drill bit and drill

DIRECTIONS

1. Drill a hole about one-third of the way from the top of the bottle and wash the bottle thoroughly.

2. Insert a short length of aquarium tubing into the hole to be used as the mouthpiece.

3. Fill the bottle one-third of the way with water and place the slide in the top.

The Double Decker Bong

This double-chambered vertical bong is easy to hold and provides a second filtering chamber to cool and filter your smoke.

BUILD TIME ✳ 20 MINUTES

MATERIALS

2 plastic water bottles (20-ounce bottles or larger work well)
Male/female slide set (see page 36)
Aquarium tubing
Duct tape
Teflon tape
Drill

85

DIRECTIONS ·····························➤

1. Remove the cap from one of the bottles. Cut off the bottom of this bottle and set it aside.
2. Drill a hole in the center of the cap of the second bottle.
3. Feed the tubing through the cap of the second bottle.
4. Create a hole one-third of the way from the bottom of the second bottle.
5. Insert the slide set into this hole.
6. Fill the second bottle with water so that the stem of the slide is submerged.
7. Place the cap with the tube back on the bottle.
8. Place the first bottle (without the bottom) on top of the second bottle so that the seal is secure.
9. Wrap a layer of Teflon tape around where the two bottles meet.
10. Then wrap a layer of duct tape around the same area.
11. Fill the top bottle with enough water so that the vinyl tube end is submerged.

The Gator Bong

This one is so refreshing! Take a second to reflect before throwing away that empty bottle. A few strategically placed holes, a DIY bowl piece, and some plastic tubing are all it takes to consider yourself a master recycler.

BUILD TIME * 15 MINUTES

MATERIALS

32-ounce plastic bottle with cap
Aquarium tubing
Thread seal tape
Bowl piece

1. Create three holes with a razor or scissors: one in the center of the bottle cap, one about a one-quarter of the way down the bottle, and one about half way down the bottle on the opposite side.

2. Feed two short lengths of tubing through the holes in the bottle, wrapping the section going through the bottle with thread seal tape.

3. Feed a longer tube through the hole in the cap.

4. Attach the bowl piece to the tube sticking out of the top of the cap, wrap a small amount of thread seal tape on the tube, and twist and push down into the cap for an airtight seal.

The Aluminum Can Pipe

You don't need much to start smoking. Grab an empty cola can and a pushpin and you're ready to go. We cannot recommend smoking through aluminum so use at your own risk! At least scrape the paint off before using.

BUILD TIME ✳ 3 MINUTES

MATERIALS

Aluminum can
Pushpin

DIRECTIONS

1. Empty and clean the can. Remove the paint from the bottom of the can if you wish.
2. Flatten the bottom portion (furthest from mouth) of one side of the can.
3. Poke holes with the pushpin in the flattened section to create the bowl airway.
4. Make a small carb hole at the bowl end of the can. Where you'd drink is now where you'll smoke!

The Can Bong

This slight modification to the can pipe turns any cola can into a functional water pipe. When you're done smoking, simply rinse and recycle.

BUILD TIME ✳ 5 MINUTES

MATERIALS

12-ounce cola can
Smoke 'n' Poke (see page 38)
Duct tape

DIRECTIONS

1. Fill the can one-third full with water.

2. Place a square of duct tape half way up the can.

3. Insert the Poke 'n' Smoke (or a homemade alternative) into the can through the duct tape. Make sure the Poke 'n' Smoke is at an angle so it goes into the water below it.

4. Make a small hole above the water line to use as a carb. Once again, where you'd drink is now where you'll smoke.

The Paper Roll Bowl

Here's a simple bowl you can make while sitting in your living room. All you need is an aluminum can, a paper towel roll tube, and a screen. One end of the tube is the mouthpiece, while the other is the rush hole. See how to make an aluminum funnel on page 155 to get started.

BUILD TIME
2 MINUTES WITH PREFABRICATED FUNNEL

101

Paper towel roll tube
Aluminum cola can
Screen

DIRECTIONS

1. See how to make an aluminum funnel on page 155.
2. Create a small hole near one end of the tube.
3. Place the funnel with the screen in it in the small hole.

The Double-Chamber Bottle Bong

This fun bong looks like some kid's middle-school science experiment, but this contraption is strictly adults only.

BUILD TIME ✷ 15 MINUTES

MATERIALS

2 bottles, 2 liters
2 pieces of aquarium tubing
Bowl piece
Screen
Elbow conduit
Duct tape
Teflon tape
Drill

DIRECTIONS

1. Create a hole in bottle #1 about halfway down.
2. Create a hole in bottle #2 in the same location.
3. Run a piece of tubing through the two holes you just created. Make sure that in bottle #1 it reaches the bottom and in bottle #2 it just barely enters.
4. Use Teflon tape for an airtight seal.

5. Drill a hole in the center of bottle #2's cap.
6. Attach your bowl piece to the second piece of tubing and feed it through the cap hole using Teflon tape to seal.
7. Remove bottle #1's cap and place the elbow conduit in the top cap hole. Begin experiment and repeat as necessary.

▼ Five Ways To

DISGUISE/HIDE YOUR BONG
(FOR WHEN YOUR MOM COMES OVER)

FLOWER VASE

Throw a couple flowers in your pipe with the bowl facing the wall and most people will never look twice.

MUSICAL INSTRUMENT

If you can make a sound out of it, you've got a shot.

LAMP

Throw a shade over your bong and hope no one needs a reading lamp.

PLANTER

Throw your favorite plant on top of your pipe in the mouthpiece. Just don't forget to water it.

TOOTHBRUSH HOLDER

Stick your pipe in your bathroom and put your toothbrushes in it.

Covert Operations

Kazoo

Here's an easy stealth pipe that's always good on the go. Simply grab a metal kazoo and a screen. Don't forget to remove the plastic filament in the kazoo before using. The larger end is your mouthpiece and the smaller your carb. It may be a good idea to have a second working kazoo around because you just might get the urge to hum a little ditty after your smoke.

BUILD TIME
30 SECONDS, IF ALREADY
LIT—OTHERWISE, 15 SECONDS

113

Metal kazoo
Screen

DIRECTIONS

1. Remove the kazoo's plastic filament and replace it with the metal screen.

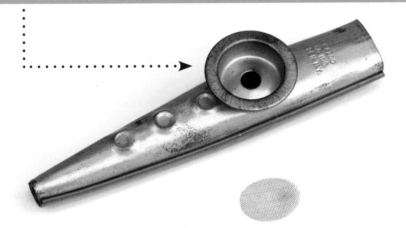

007 Prescription Bong

On the go? On the down low? This pipe's components neatly break down and can be stored within the prescription bottle. There are a couple of required holes that can be made before travel or after. Add a little water and you're ready to go.

BUILD TIME ❋ 10 MINUTES

MATERIALS

Prescription bottle
Half of a hollow pen shaft
Short length of aquarium tubing
Bowl piece
Screen
Teflon tape
Drill

DIRECTIONS

1. Fill the bottle about one-third full with water.
2. Create a hole in the center of the cap.
3. Connect the tubing to the bowl piece.
4. Feed the tubing through the cap hole.

5. Wrap the threads of the bowl in Teflon tape and screw through the hole in the cap, creating an airtight seal.
6. Create a second hole near the top of the bottle for the carb.
7. Secure the pen shaft piece in the second hole.
8. Place the screen in the bowl piece, and you're ready for your medicine.

 Covert AND compact—perfect for when you're on the
go and want to bring your medication with you.

Coffee Drinker's Bong

Waking up in the morning can be tough. But looking forward to this treat may just help get you on your feet.

BUILD TIME ✳ 5 MINUTES

Large paper coffee cup with top
Bowl piece
Screen
Short length of aquarium tubing
Teflon tape

DIRECTIONS ◄••••••••••••••••••••••••••••••••

1. Create a hole about one-third from the bottom of the cup. Fill the cup up to the hole with water.
2. Connect the tubing to the bowl piece and feed it through the hole—make sure the tubing enters the water.
3. Wrap the bowl and tubing with Teflon tape to seal. Put the screen in the bowl piece.
4. Use the lid as the mouthpiece.

Vase Bong

You can keep this water pipe on display without fear of non-smokers recognizing it for what it is. Simply put a few flowers in it and no one will ever know. You'll need a diamond-coated drill bit to make your holes in the glass.

BUILD TIME ✳ 15 MINUTES

127

MATERIALS

Glass vase with narrow opening
2 pieces of aquarium tubing, one shorter than the other
Bowl piece
Diamond-coated drill bit
Drill

DIRECTIONS

1. Carefully drill two holes in the vase on opposite sides. The front hole, for the bowl piece, should be slightly higher than the back carb hole.

2. Feed the short length of tubing into the back hole so just a little protrudes.

3. Connect the longer length of tubing to the bowl piece and feed it through the front hole.

4. Fill the vase with enough water so that the bowl piece's tubing is submerged in the water.

HIDE POT SMOKE

THE DRYER-SHEET TUBE

Grab a cardboard paper towel roll and stuff a dryer sheet into one end. Exhale your smoke into the other end, allowing the smoke to pass through the dryer sheet's fragrance.

TOWEL THE DOOR

Roll up a towel and line the bottom of your door with it to stop the smoke from flowing out.

THE STEAMING COVER-UP

Get in the shower and crank up the heat. The steam will serve as the perfect cover for your smoke. Be careful not to burn yourself.

INCENSE

It may alert people to your true hippie nature, but incense is a great aromatic cover-up.

PVC EXHAUST PIPE

Pick up a couple feet of PVC pipe. Keep an end out a slightly open window and exhale through the tube.

Unique & Peculiar

Didgeridoo Rush Tube

This one is for the extreme musician who wants a rush like no other. This is a two-person operation, as you'll need a friend at the other end to light the joint and help you support it. This will burn through joints pretty quickly, so be warned.

BUILD TIME
1 MINUTE WITH PREFABRICATED
JOINT FUNNEL

MATERIALS

Joint
Joint funnel (see page 158)
Didgeridoo
A friend

DIRECTIONS

1. Create a joint funnel—directions on page 158.

2. Have your friend stand at the bowl end while you stand at the other end with your mouth on the hole.

3. Have your friend light the joint while you inhale lightly.

4. After the joint is lit, draw a big breath to fill the didgeridoo with smoke. Then give your friend the signal to remove the funnel. (We suggest a grunt of some type since your mouth will be on the tube.) Then inhale as hard as you can.

Note: You can substitute any long cylindrical object you can get your hands on, such as a PVC pipe.

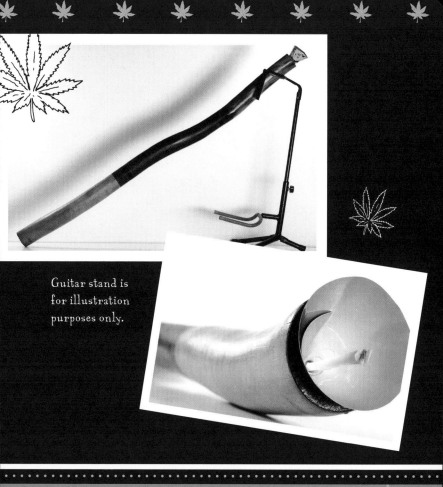

Guitar stand is
for illustration
purposes only.

The Waterfall Bong

This variation of the gravity bong is lots of fun. You'll need to set up somewhere that you can spill water, such as a shower or outside.

BUILD TIME ✳ 10 MINUTES

MATERIALS

Plastic bottle with bottle cap
Poke 'n' Smoke (see page 38)
Teflon tape
Drill

DIRECTIONS

1. Drill a hole in the center of the bottle cap.
2. Insert the Poke 'n' Smoke into the hole in the bottle cap.
3. Use Teflon tape to make an airtight seal.
4. While the bottle is empty, make a small hole you can cover with your finger at the base of the bottle.
5. Remove the cap and keep your finger over the hole at the base of the bottle while you fill the bottle with water.
6. Screw the cap with the Poke 'n' Smoke inserted back on.
7. Fill the bowl of the Poke 'n' Smoke and hold a flame above the bowl.
8. Remove your finger from the hole.
9. As the water drains, smoke will be drawn into the bottle. Continue until all the water is drained.
10. Remove the cap and inhale.

The Milk Jug Gravity Bong

This classic is sure to give you a head rush. Don't try anything too athletic immediately after use.

BUILD TIME ✳ 5 MINUTES

MATERIALS

Milk jug
Bucket
Bowl piece
Screen
Teflon tape

DIRECTIONS ·······························▶

1. Cut the bottom off the milk jug.
2. Make a hole in the milk jug lid for your bowl piece, secure it, and make sure it's airtight by using Teflon tape around the hole.
3. Fill bucket with water.
4. Submerge the milk jug so that just the top portion is above the water.
5. Light the bowl as you slowly raise the milk jug out of the bucket.
6. Continue raising the jug until it's just barely submerged in the water.
7. Take the cap off and immediately cover the open top with your mouth.
8. Slowly lower the jug back into the water as you inhale.

The Four-Man Hookah Bong

Got some friends coming over? This is a great one for chilling in the living room. It works best if everyone draws in his or her breath with the same amount of force. Practice makes perfect.

BUILD TIME ✳ 30 MINUTES

MATERIALS ▸

4 small water bottles
Larger bottle made out of thicker plastic, such as a pretzel jar
Bowl piece
Screen

16-inch piece of aquarium tubing
4 pieces of aquarium tubing, 24-inches long
4 pieces of aquarium tubing, 8-inches long
Duct tape
Drill

DIRECTIONS ·······················➤

1. Make four holes halfway up the large bottle. Make sure they're equidistant from each other.

2. Place a square piece of duct tape over each hole.

3. Make a hole in each of the four smaller water bottles slightly higher than those on the big bottle.

4. Place a square of duct tape over each hole.

5. Connect each small bottle with one of the four 8-inch pieces of tubing to the large bottle. Push the tubing through the duct tape to create a seal.

6. Make a hole in the center of the four small bottles' caps and feed a piece of 24-inch tubing into each.

7. Make a hole in the center of the large bottle's lid.

8. Connect the 16-inch tube to the bowl and feed it through the large lid so the tube is hanging down into the bottle.

9. Fill the small water bottles halfway so that the tubes from the large bottle are submerged.

10. Fill the main chamber so the tube from the bowl piece is submerged, but not the four tubes coming from the smaller bottles. Time to party.

The Traffic Cone
Emergency Gravity Bong

Have an urge for an emergency gravity bong rip? Grab a parking cone and head toward your tub (or a vessel deep and wide enough for the cone to mostly submerge). You'll also need the top half of a plastic bottle (32-ounce bottle works well), and the bottle cap with your bowl piece attached.

BUILD TIME ✳ 5 MINUTES

Traffic cone
32-ounce bottle
Bowl piece
Screen
Bathtub (not pictured)
Drill

DIRECTIONS ·······································

1. Cut the top one-third of the 32-ounce bottle.
2. Create a hole in the center of the bottle cap.
3. Twist the bowl piece through the hole in the bottle cap.
4. Place the bottle top over the traffic cone's hole.
5. Head to a bathtub and fill it with water.
6. Submerge the cone so that just the top portion is sticking out of the water.

7. Hold a flame over the bowl piece as you or a friend slowly raise the cone out of the water, until just the base is still submerged.
8. Remove the bottle/bowl and immediately cover the cone hole with your mouth.
9. Lower the cone back into the water as you inhale.

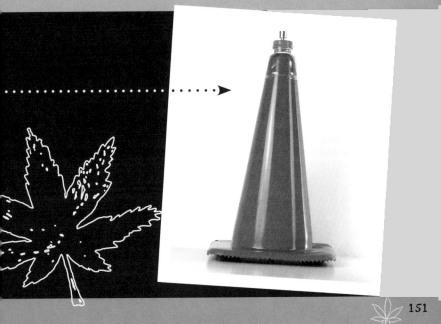

GLASSBLOWING

Glass has been used to fashion objects for much of history, with artifacts dating all the way back to 3,500 years ago. There are many hypotheses as to when glass objects were first produced, but relics exist from the pre-Roman era. The big advancement in glass production happened around 50 BCE in the Roman Empire when the discovery of "glassblowing" first took form. Instead of creating an object from the inside out with a core, craftsmen were able to shape the glass into vessels. Glass relics have also been found in China and the Middle East. Modern-day glass bongs would not be possible without the invention of glassblowing.

COLOR-CHANGING GLASS

Want to buy a pipe that will develop over time and transform into an even more beautiful piece of art? Glassblowers often use a process called "fuming" to create a color-changing pipe. They burn gold and silver alloys and let the vapors pass through the hot glass. Metal ions attach to the glass. As smoke passes through the pipe, resin is deposited. The resin, which is black, provides a backdrop for the ions within the glass and the colors emerge. Want to start the process over? Just clean the pipe.

153

Extras, Extras

Aluminum Funnel Bowl

The funnel bowl can be used as a bowl with a variety of other materials, such as the Paper Roll Bowl (page 100).

BUILD TIME ☀ 10 MINUTES

MATERIALS ◄····················

Cola can
Tin snips or scissors
Screen
Duct tape

DIRECTIONS ◄ ·

1. Cut the cola can in half and then cut a circular disc out of one half of the can.
2. Cut a straight line from one edge of the disc to the center of it.
3. At the center, cut a hole that's small enough for the screen to cover it.
4. Twist the disc into a cone shape and apply a little force until it maintains the funnel shape. (The aluminum is fairly moldable.) Feel free to use a little duct tape to get the funnel to hold its shape. Put the screen in the funnel so you don't eat your treat.

Joint Funnel

The joint funnel serves several purposes and can be used in a variety of pipes, such as the Didgeridoo Rush Tube on page 133. The beauty of this piece is that it holds the joint securely while catching all the ash. It's also good for solving debates between joint smokers and pipe smokers.

BUILD TIME ✳ 20 MINUTES

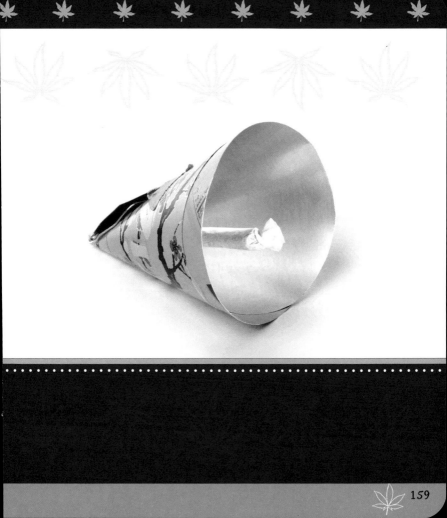

Cola can
2 metal paperclips
Pencil
Duct tape
Pliers

DIRECTIONS

1. First, make a Aluminum Funnel Bowl (page 155). Make sure this funnel is a least the length of your average joint, so you may want to use a bigger can.

2. After making the funnel, take a metal paperclip and wrap it around the pencil, creating a spiral Remove the spiral from the pencil.

3. Take the second paperclip and straighten it except for one curved hook.

4. Connect the base of the spiral paperclip to the hook of second paperclip and twist and crimp with pliers so they interlock.

5. Take the combined paperclips and feed the straight end through the center of the funnel so the spiral is resting inside the funnel and the straight paperclip is sticking out through the funnel's hole.

6. Bend the straight portion of the paperclip up into the fold of the cone and tape it using duct tape.

Tin Foil Bowl

This is the ultimate disposable, on-the-go, pipe. You don't need much to make it — just a rectangular 5 x 3-inch sheet of aluminum foil and a hollow pen shaft.

BUILD TIME ✳ 5 MINUTES

MATERIALS ◄ • • • • • • • • • • • • • • • • • •

Aluminum foil
Hollow pen shaft

DIRECTIONS ◄ ·······························

1. Cut the foil to 5 x 3 inches. The foil needs to be slightly longer than the pen shaft, so either cut the foil or the pen shaft to fit.

2. Place the pen shaft at one end of the flat foil and roll it up into a tube.

3. Pull the pen out until just an inch is still inside the foil. Carefully bend the portion still around the pen to a 90-degree angle to the rest of the foil tube.

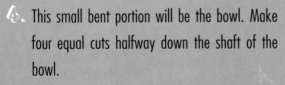

4. This small bent portion will be the bowl. Make four equal cuts halfway down the shaft of the bowl.

5. Fold the bowl strips you just cut into your own decorative pattern.

Common Names for Pipes and Bongs

Piece
Bowl
Chillum
Oney
One-hitter
Bat
Dugout

167

Awesome Bongs from the

PERSONAL COLLECTION OF DR. SEYMOUR KINDBUD

THE GLASS APPLE

Dr. Kindbud ran into this beauty in a New Hampshire head shop and declared it must be added to his collection. Although this is not a water pipe, its beauty warranted placement in this book.

THE GLASS BUBBLER

Here's a classic color-changing glass bubbler—one of Dr. Seymour Kindbud's favorites.

THE BONG-SHAPED BUBBLER

Here's a great piece that uses the standard bong shape but doesn't have a slide. Instead it utilizes a carb hole at the back of the pipe.

THE CLASSIC CORNCOB PIPE

Embrace your country roots and enjoy a smoke out of this timeless pipe.

PARTY GAMES

Smoking Games

Most games can be converted into smoking games if you put a little thought into it. Take a cue from your alcoholic brethren who have so diligently adapted both board and card games into drinking games and do the same with herb.

Themes

The Green Party

People are always throwing parties with tons of alcohol, which lends itself to a certain type of outcome. Try switching it up with a green party and see where the night takes you. Of course it's fine to have a green party with supplemental alcohol for social lubrication. Key elements for an awesome green party include:

Music: You'll want a playlist of your favorite atmospheric tunes to expand your guest's minds.

Munchies: You'll absolutely need a steady supply of munchies. A trip to your grocer's frozen-food aisle, and some healthy alternatives like pita and hummus, should keep everyone satisfied.

The Distraction Batch: This is a very clever move known only to master party throwers. For this example we will use nachos, but use your imagination. Confidently tell your guests you're going to prepare a dish of nachos in the kitchen. Subtly signal a few of your closest friends to give you a hand. Once in the kitchen, make two batches of nachos. Heat up the first batch. Once that batch is done, begin heating the second batch while your friends take out the first to the guests. They will all be so consumed with the delicious treat in front of them, no one will notice you and a few friends are missing. You will be in another room sophisticatedly sharing a generous portion while the guests scramble to get theirs.

The Stoner Scavenger Hunt

Get stoned and compete with friends! Here is a scavenger hunt that's sure to bring some (mis)adventure to your baked life. This list should be used as a starting point. Feel free to make up your own list that suit your party. Players compete to fulfill the following tasks and collect the following items. First one to finish wins. Not being incredibly stoned is considered cheating! Keep your pockets clean while out though, or you may not return for the win.

Scavenger Hunt List:

- Everyone find your keys and store them on your person for safekeeping.
- Enter a restaurant, fill out a job application, and get the manager's business card.
- Convince a stranger on the street to give you his or her autograph.
- Find a used piece of paper and create origami. (There's more than one way to be green!)

- Go to your local hardware store and get the fixings to create your own pipe. Do not assemble it in the store.
- Meet up with all participants at a private location to "revitalize" your scavenger senses and build your pipes.
- Everyone find your keys! Back out on the street.
- Get a stranger to take a picture with you.
- Ask a cop to write down directions to a location of your choosing.
- Make it home safely.

That's quite a list of accomplishments!

INSPIRATIONS

Some people find inspiration in dark places. I guess I'm one of them. What always made me different is that if I was doing drugs I was also making music. I wasn't just doing drugs.
-Lady Gaga

I don't have a stance on it. I enjoy it ... not while I'm pregnant, obviously. I'm all about moderation— as best I can be. As an artist, there's a sweet jump-starting quality to it for me.

-Alanis Morissette

I enjoy smoking cannabis and see no harm in it.
-Jennifer Aniston

184

If John Lennon is deported, I'm leaving too ... with my musicians ... and my marijuana.

-Art Garfunkel

If the words "life, liberty and the pursuit of happiness" don't include the right to experiment with your own consciousness, then the Declaration of Independence isn't worth the hemp it was written on.

-Terence McKenna

It really puzzles me to see marijuana connected with narcotics . . . dope and all that crap. It's a thousand times better than whiskey. It's an assistant ... a friend.

-Louis Armstrong

I think pot should be legal. I don't smoke it, but I like the smell of it.

-Andy Warhol ◄ • • • • • • • • • • • • •

We shall, by and by, want a world of hemp more for our own consumption.

-John Adams

• • • • • • • • • •

I wondered, "Would being stoned look way better on the film than acting stoned?"

-Edward Norton on making the film *Leaves of Grass*

Kyle Gass: I think the very last scene we had a good time when we're smoking out of the Devil's bong. We put some real pot in there.

Jack Black: Yeah. I got too high and I was paranoid that there were some SAG secret officials there that were gonna bust us for smoking real pot. It's too powerful. Someone put the chronic in there. Two bong hits. I'm a lightweight, too, so it's like, "Aaaaaaaah." Driving home was a real challenge.

-Tenacious D

Let's get to the point,
Let's roll another joint.

-Tom Petty, "You Don't Know How it Feels"

President Bush needs to smoke marijuana. @#$% Bush!

-Wycelf Jean

Two of my favorite things are sitting on my front porch smoking a pipe of sweet hemp, and playing my Hohner harmonica.

-Abraham Lincoln (from a letter written by Lincoln during his presidency to the head of the Hohner Harmonica Company in Germany)

I went through one period when I smoked a surprising, a really breathtaking, amount of grass almost every night.

-David Letterman

Forty percent of the U.S. population has tried pot—that's 94 million Americans. Or as I call them—my base. Are we all criminals? No, we're not. But it is criminal when a certain person borrows and doesn't return another person's diamond-encrusted bong, Woody! [referring to fellow Celeb Stoner Woody Harrelson]

-Bill Maher

Let us burn one from end to end,
and pass it over to me my friend.

-Ben Harper, "Burn One Down"

Hemp is of first necessity to the wealth & protection of the country.

-Thomas Jefferson

I love you more than my after-show monster bong hit...

-Sarah Silverman, "Jesus is Magic"

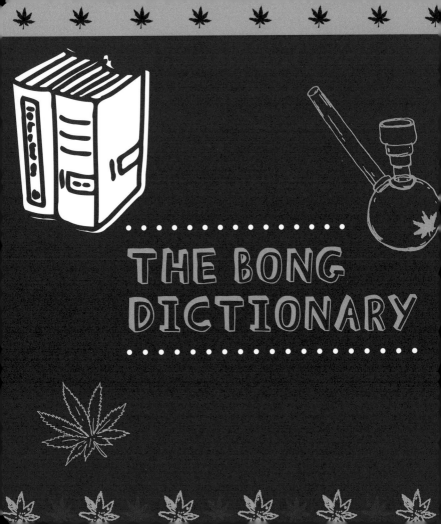

THE BONG
DICTIONARY

Ash Catcher: 1. A secondary water-filled chamber that slides in and out of the main chamber, providing extra filtering and prevention of ash entering the main chamber. 2. A cone that allows joints to be smoked hands-free without ash falling on the floor.

. . . .

Bong: A pipe comprised of a water-holding chamber, a bowl whose stem goes into the water, and a mouthpiece to inhale through.

. . . .

Bogart: To mindlessly hold onto a smoking device without regard to others anxiously waiting their turn.

. . . .

Carb: Short for carburetor. A secondary hole used to clear the bong or pipe by allowing fresh air to rush through. Also known as a rush hole.

. . . .

Cashed: A bowl in which its contents have been completely used.

. . . .

Chillum: A small pipe usually used for covert smoking. Generally chillums are a straight shot from the bowl to the mouthpiece with no added extras. Also known as an oney, one-hitter, bat, or dugout.

. . . .

Clearing: Drawing fresh air into the chamber in order to clear all the smoke out.

. . . .

Diffuser: A slide with a sealed bottom with tiny holes in it. This serves to break the smoke into smaller bubbles within the water. This provides more smoke filtering and a cooler smoke.

. . . .

Fuming: The process in which a glassblower allows ions from burning gold and silver to penetrate the glass, which creates a "color changing" piece.

Hit: an inhalation of smoke.

Head shop: A store where pipes and tobacco-related accessories are sold.

Hookah: A tobacco pipe originating from the East in which smoke is drawn through a chamber with water in it and into a long tube with a mouthpiece at the end.

Ice catcher: A shelf or lip in a pipe chamber that holds ice cubes for cool smoking.

. . . .

Percolator: A secondary chamber filled with water that filters and cools the water a second time.

. . . .

Piece: An alternate name for a pipe.

. . . .

Resin: A sticky black substance that results as a byproduct of burning herbs. After a few uses, resin buildup will be noticeable in a pipe, eventually leading to clogging if it's not scraped or cleaned.

. . . .

Rush tube: A pipe that's whole tubular chamber acts as a rush hole — such as a didgeridoo.

Screen: The small circular screen that's used to put in the bowl component of a pipe to stop your product from being sucked through.

. . . .

Session: A group of people enjoying a smoke together.

. . . .

Slide: A slide is made up of two parts, a male and a female. The female piece secures to the pipe while the male easily slides into it creating an airtight seal. The slide is very useful because it serves as a carb to clear the smoke as well as the bowl piece.

. . . .

THC: Stands for *tetrahydrocannabinol* and it's the main active ingredient in marijuana.

. . . .

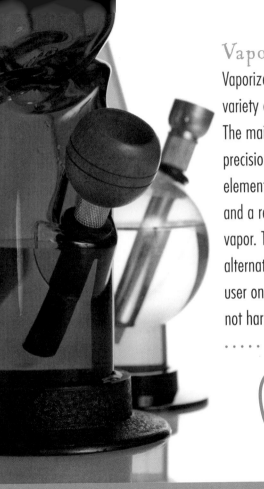

Vaporizer:

Vaporizers come in a variety of shapes and sizes. The main elements are a precision-controlled heating element attached to a bowl and a receptacle to hold the vapor. This is a healthier alternative to a bong and the user only inhales vapor and not harmful smoke.

. . . .

REFERENCES & RESOURCES

Want to get into the cannabis market professionally? Check out Oaksterdam University.
www.oaksterdamuniversity.com

Stay up to date with what's going on in pot land at:
 www.rollitup.org

Let your voice be heard or hear other's at the Stoner Forums.
www.stonerforums.com

Stash Cans: Great for traveling on the road or hiding at home.
www.misdefenseproducts.com

For a great history of glassblowing check out the following link.
www.glassblowing.com

Want to become a glassblower? Check out the Revere Glass School in Berkley, California.
www.revereglass.com

Bong Vodka: Enjoy some cocktails with your friends and then transform the empty bottle into a bong to keep the party going.
www.bongspirit.com/bong

Purple Power Liquid Glass Cleaner is great for cleaning your pipes and restoring them to their original state. You can buy it from many head shops and online outlets such as www.groovy-glass.com.

NOTES

_____

_____

_____

_____

_____

_____

_____

_____

_____

_____

ABOUT
CIDER MILL PRESS

Good ideas ripen with time. From seed to harvest, Cider Mill Press brings fine reading, information, and entertainment together between the covers of its creatively crafted books. Our Cider Mill bears fruit twice a year, publishing a new crop of titles each spring and fall.

Visit us on the Web at
www.cidermillpress.com
or write to us at
12 Port Farm Road
Kennebunkport, Maine 04046